football's new wave

Terrell Davis

Toughing It Out

By
Mark Stewart

THE MILLBROOK PRESS
BROOKFIELD, CONNECTICUT

M

THE MILLBROOK PRESS

Produced by
BITTERSWEET PUBLISHING
John Sammis, President
and
TEAM STEWART, INC.

Series Design and Electronic Page Makeup by
JAFFE ENTERPRISES
Ron Jaffe

Researched and Edited by
Mariah Morgan

All photos courtesy
AP/ Wide World Photos, Inc.
except the following:
Tony Tomsic/SportsChrome — Cover
Long Beach State — Pages 13, 15
University of Georgia — Pages 16, 18

Printed in the United States of America

Published by
The Millbrook Press, Inc.
2 Old New Milford Road
Brookfield, Connecticut   06804

Visit us at our Web site – http://www.millbrookpress.com

Library of Congress Cataloging-in-Publication Data

Stewart, Mark.
    Terrell Davis: toughing it out / by Mark Stewart
    p.   cm.   — (Football's new wave)
    Includes index.
    Summary: An illustrated biography of the Denver Broncos running back who is emerging as one of the
all-purpose offensive powers in the National Football League.
    ISBN 0-7613-1514-4 (lib. bdg.)   ISBN 0-7613-1038-X (pbk.)
    1. Davis, Terrell, 1972– —Juvenile literature. Football players—United States—Biography—Juvenile
literature. 3. Denver Broncos (Football team)—Juvenile literature. [1. Davis, Terrell, 1972– . 2. Football
players. 3. Afro-Americans—Biography.] I. Title. II. Series.
GV939.D347S84   1999
796.332'092--dc21
[b]   99-17952
                                                                                                  CIP

pbk: 1 3 5 7 9 10 8 6 4 2
lib: 1 3 5 7 9 10 8 6 4 2

Contents

Chapter   Page

Dealing with Dad

"I thought I'd have a houseful of kids and we'd all go to church on Sunday and I'd cook dinner every night and my husband would say, 'Hi, honey, I'm home!'"

— **KATEREE DAVIS**

Kateree Davis and her five sons boarded a Greyhound bus in St. Louis in September of 1972. She hoped her family was headed for a new beginning. Their destination was San Diego, California, a place where the sun was always shining and her husband, Joe, could wipe the slate clean. He joined her a month later, in time to witness the birth of his sixth son, Terrell.

Joe Davis had spent much of his life in prison, doing time for armed robbery and grand theft. A welder by trade, he had problems with alcohol and drugs and was rarely able to hold down a job for very long. Even after the fresh start in California, Joe eventually went back to his old ways. As Terrell grew up, he often found items in the house he knew did not belong to his father, such as televisions and stereos. And danger

Terrell has come a long way from his troubled childhood in San Diego. His long, twisting path to stardom is one of the most inspiring stories in sports.

always seemed seconds away. "When it came to living with my pops, my brothers and I saw guns so often," he recalls, "it became as routine as seeing the ice cream truck."

Eight years after moving their family to San Diego, Joe and Kateree separated. After that, Kateree lived with her two oldest sons—James and Joe, Jr.—in a place on Latimer Street, while Joe and the four youngest—Reggie, Bobby, Terry, and Terrell—lived in a tiny house on Florence Street. It was closer to the boys' school, and Joe could be home in the evenings for the kids. On the weekends, all the kids stayed with mom. It was not a perfect setup, but then perfection was not a concept with which the Davis boys were familiar. Terrell missed his mother, especially at night, when his father stumbled into the house after a night of drinking.

Did You Know?

Terrell got his name from his mom's favorite singer, Tammi Terrell.

When Joe was drunk or on drugs, the boys never knew what to expect. Once, he woke them up and told them their new puppies were making too much noise. He dressed the kids and led them on a forced march through the neighborhood, dropping puppies into neighbors' yards in the dead of night. On another occasion, Joe lined his four youngest sons up against a wall, pulled out a pistol, and fired shots above their heads to see how tough they were. Sometimes, Joe came home and brought his violent world with him, like the time someone came looking for revenge and emptied a shotgun into the side of the house. Terrell remembers waking up that night to find a swarm of police officers in his room with their guns drawn and their flashlights shining in his eyes.

As it turned out, this incident really shook Joe up. It was one thing to put his own life on the line, but to risk the lives of his children was unacceptable. From that point on, he managed to stay out of serious trouble, and concentrated more on being a good father. He still ruled over Terrell and his brothers with a firm hand—and he still got drunk a lot—but on balance, the Davis boys remember him being a fairly good father.

Terrell's mother worked hard and did what she could to keep her sons safe from the terrors on both sides of the front door. Married at 16 after dropping out of high school, she got her equivalency diploma, took a job as a nurse's aide, and studied at San Diego City College to become a nurse. She would make breakfast and dinner for the children each morning, and then reappear around midnight after double-shifts at work and school and studying. "I never saw anyone with so much energy," remembers Terrell.

One day, the four youngest Davis brothers were playing baseball when a friend of their mother's picked them up and drove them to the hospital. Kateree was there, crying. Joe, who had been suffering from lupus for several years, never liked to take his medication, and that day he had collapsed and died. Terrell, 14, did not know what to feel. He despised his father for the pain and violence he brought upon his family. But he loved him, too.

"I still remember looking at pops the day he died," says Terrell. "All life just came out of me."

Terrell embraces his mother at a ceremony to retire his high-school number. Kateree Davis's endless energy and devotion to her family have inspired Terrell throughout his life.

Terrell now talks openly about the blinding headaches that
have plagued him for 20 years. Not until college, however,
was his condition correctly diagnosed.

Lonely Boy in a Dark Room

"I remember thinking, is this how it happens for blind people?"

— **TERRELL DAVIS**

From the time he could pick up a ball and run, Terrell loved to play football. He was big for his age—he weighed 90 pounds (40 kg) on his seventh birthday—and his friends called him "Boss Hogg," after a rotund character on the television show *Dukes of Hazzard*. Needless to say, Terrell was not an easy kid to bring down. In Pop Warner football, he routinely rushed for 300 to 400 yards per game. Naturally, other teams would shout, "Look out for number 30!" before plays started, and the defenders would converge on Terrell. To combat this strategy, his coach would give him a jersey with a different number on it at halftime. The trick usually worked only a play or two—when number 32 or 33 galloped 50 yards for a touchdown, the other team usually figured out they had been fooled.

One night after practice, Terrell was waiting for his mother to come pick him up, when his eyes began playing tricks on him. Everything was all mixed up, and he could barely make out the figures on the football field. "I was like, man, I'm going blind," he says. "I was praying to the Lord, *Please this can't be happening.*"

Terrell's vision cleared by the time his mom arrived, but he was soon overwhelmed by a headache so intense that it seemed to radiate from deep inside his brain. Nothing helped, and for several hours all he did was moan and throw up. The waves of pain finally subsided around three or four in the morning. These episodes continued, several times a year, throughout his childhood. Doctors tested Terrell but could find nothing wrong and could prescribe no medication. He believed that the headaches were caused by exposure to bright light, so he tried to stay out of the sun and sleep as much as possible. When the attacks occurred, all he could do was ride them out—alone, in a dark room, with a bucket nearby. "I don't want to live!" he would scream. "I can't stand it!"

The episodes did not keep Terrell from playing sports or hanging out with his friends, but they dampened his enthusiasm for life. It was difficult to wake up each day wondering if this was going to be "one of those days."

Not surprisingly, when Joe Davis died, Terrell hit rock bottom. Life, he felt, was hammering on him from every conceivable direction. For a while, he just stopped caring. Terrell stopped playing football, choosing to spend his afternoons and evenings in the company of gang members and drug dealers. For two years, Terrell's mother watched helplessly as he slipped away.

"The only thing I can tell you is it's like a collage—like if you've got a bunch of pictures and you cut them up and put them on a board. A million pictures on a board. Stuff is everywhere."

TERRELL DAVIS, PICTURED HERE PARTICIPATING IN A SEMINAR ON MIGRAINE HEADACHES, ON WHAT HE SEES DURING ONE OF HIS ATTACKS.

Jamaul

chapter

> *"My teachers couldn't stand me.
> I can't blame them."*
>
> — **TERRELL DAVIS**

An excellent student before his father's passing, Terrell began skipping school as much as he went. When he did show up in class, he was often late or disruptive. It got to the point where he could not have played football had he wanted to, for his grades were abysmal. After missing what should have been his freshman and sophomore seasons on the Morse High School football team, Terrell was regarded as just another promising athlete on his way to nowhere. The streets of San Diego's Skyline district were full of kids like that.

The person who brought Terrell back was his best friend, Jamaul Pennington. The two walked and talked and thought alike—in fact, they were so tight that most people assumed they were cousins. Jamaul had moved into the Davis home when his mother could no longer afford to support him, and he and Terrell spent practically every waking moment together. The two teenagers talked of opening a nightclub together someday or becoming partners in some other business.

Jamaul pointed out to Terrell that he had to do something about his grades if he planned to go anywhere in life. He also pointed out that Terrell's reputation was ruined at Morse. Toward the end of sophomore year, Terrell applied for and received a trans-

fer to Lincoln Prep Academy. He attended summer classes to make up for all of the Fs he had accumulated at Morse, and practically lived in the library his junior year. "Lincoln was where I always wanted to go anyway," Terrell says. "I liked the teachers and got involved in extracurricular activities."

Terrell's academic turnaround made him eligible to play for the Lincoln football team, which ranked among the best in Southern California. Marcus Allen, one of the greatest runners in NFL history, had attended Lincoln during the 1970s, so naturally everyone on the team wanted to be a running back. When Terrell got to tryouts, he found his old position crowded with kids who had already been in Coach Vic Player's system for two and three years. No problem, Terrell thought, I'll just go out for nose tackle. It had been three years since he had pulled on a jersey, so his goal was simply to get into the lineup.

Jamaul videotaped Terrell in practice, and they watched the films together. Soon Terrell was one of the squad's top defensive players. Later that season, he also became the team's kicker. In all, he played six different positions during his two years at Lincoln, including running back. As a senior, he gained 700 yards and helped the team go 12–2 and advance to the city championship game. Although Terrell was voted All-League, he was not what you would call a superstar. However, he definitely had the instincts, the skills, and the toughness to move to the next level.

Terrell's brother Reggie had used football to get a college scholarship to Long Beach State, a good school located less than two hours north of San Diego. This is what he wanted to do. But having missed two seasons—and lacking the eye-popping stats that attract recruiters—Terrell seemed to have little chance of following in Reggie's footsteps. "I figured football was over for me when I finished high school," he remembers.

Terrell's brother, Reggie Webb

Bouncing Around

chapter 4

> "I told them there was a pretty good running back at Lincoln High they should take a look at...I didn't mention that he was my brother."
>
> — REGGIE WEBB

Reggie Webb was the only one of Terrell's five brothers who was not Joe Davis's son. While Joe was in prison, Kateree had had an affair with a man named Ike Webb, and nine months later Reggie was born. Joe raised him and loved him as his own, but Reggie chose to keep his biological father's name. This turned out to be a stroke of luck for Terrell.

Reggie was Long Beach State's starting tailback. The team's coach was George Allen, who had made winners out of the Rams and the Redskins during his days in the National Football League. Allen was known for playing hunches, and looking for talent where he believed others had not. Knowing this, Reggie mentioned to Allen that there was a kid named Terrell Davis who had just finished his senior year at Lincoln. The Long Beach coaches worked him out, liked what they saw, and offered Terrell an athletic scholarship. Only later did they discover that he was actually Reggie's brother!

Terrell was "red-shirted" during his first year at Long Beach (1990), practicing with the team but not playing in games. Prior to the 1991 season, Coach Allen died and was replaced by Willie Brown, a former NFL player. He used Terrell as a substitute for Reggie, and later in the season moved Reggie to fullback and used both brothers in the same backfield. Unfortunately, after the 1991 season, Long Beach State decided to drop its football program. Terrell and his teammates had a choice of staying in school and not playing football, or accepting a scholarship from another university.

UCLA, an excellent school, expressed interest in Terrell. Although the Bruins were very deep at the running back position, Terrell was inclined to go there because of the academics and because it was in Southern California. But then he received a call from the University of Georgia. "If you'd given me a puzzle of the fifty states, I wouldn't have known where to put Georgia," he laughs. "But it was a free trip, so I went."

The Georgia coaches overwhelmed Terrell when he arrived. They explained that he would be part of the school's great foot-ball tradition, and that he would be treat-ed like royalty while he was there. "They had my jersey with my name already on it," he says. "I was like, *I'm here!*"

Terrell spent the 1992 season as a backup for Garrison Hearst, who finished third in the Heisman Trophy voting that season. He did not mind sitting behind such a good player, because he knew Hearst would be drafted the following spring. Terrell believed he would then step into the role of featured ballcarrier at one of the great running schools in NCAA history—one that had produced the likes of stars Charley Trippi, Frank Sinkwich, Herschel Walker, Tim Worley, and Rodney Hampton.

Long Beach State coach George Allen

Forced to play catch-up in most games, Georgia relied more on quarterback Eric Zeier than on Terrell. Zeier was a third-round pick in the 1995 NFL draft.

In 1993, Georgia coach Ray Goff had two weapons at his disposal: Terrell's legs and the arm of quarterback Eric Zeier. The Bulldogs, however, did not have much else. Pressured to uphold Georgia's long winning tradition, Goff began taking out his frustration on his players. Terrell, who did not believe in beating himself up in practice, became the coach's favorite target. He belittled Terrell in front of his teammates, and cut him out of the offense when the team needed him most. As the season progressed, Georgia's focus moved toward the passing game, leaving Terrell out in the cold. Often, he sat on the bench when he knew he could be helping the team win. He finished the year with a respectable, but unspectacular, 824 yards. His one breakout performance came against Arkansas, when he carried the ball 31 times for 177 yards.

It was a frustrating season. A college coach can make or break a talented young player's career, and Coach Goff seemed to have it in for Terrell. Even so, some college observers ranked him among the top five pro prospects at his

Terrell rips through tacklers during his last college game, a 48–10 victory over Georgia Tech in November 1994.

position. Terrell wasn't unknown, just unused. The only positive thing about the season was that one of the team's trainers identified the headaches Terrell had been having since he was a kid: They were severe migraines. An anti-inflammatory drug called Indocin was prescribed, which greatly reduced the number of episodes.

That was the good news. The bad news was that Terrell still had the 1994 season to endure under Coach Goff. Anticipating a frustrating senior year, Terrell thought it would be nice to have some support close by. Jamaul had just completed a hitch in the Navy and had returned to San Diego. Terrell called his friend and asked him to come stay with him at Georgia. He could take some classes or just hang out—the important thing was to stay off the streets. Jamaul declined the invitation and assured Terrell that he would be fine. He had just secured a job as an electrician's apprentice, and would be learning skills that would come in handy when he and Terrell launched their nightclub, which they still talked about all the time.

A week later, Jamaul got into an argument with a man while gambling. The man pulled out a gun and shot him dead.

University of Georgia coach Ray Goff

Camp Meat

chapter

*"He'll be an okay back,
but don't expect much from him."*
— RAY GOFF

errell began his final year at Georgia wondering if anything else could go wrong in his life. He soon had an answer. In preseason camp, he felt a twinge in his left hamstring. Terrell sat out a couple of days to let it heal, but Coach Goff demanded that he practice, threatening to bench him if he did not. It was a terrible choice Terrell had to make. In his "make-or-break" college season, he either had to risk an injury that would hamper him all year, or sit on the bench while NFL scouts assumed the worst about him. Terrell decided to play.

In a game against Tennessee, the hamstring blew, knocking him out of action for nearly a month. Terrell finished the year with just 445 yards. The same pro teams that would have gladly gambled a first- or second-round pick on him a year earlier now had

Did You Know?

*Author! Author!
Terrell recently wrote a book entitled*
TD: Dreams in Motion.

serious reservations. To make matters worse, Coach Goff was hardly in Terrell's corner. "The head man there didn't go out of his way to even sit down with the scouts and tell them about my situation," Terrell complains of his former coach. "And that goes a long way, because they are going to go with who knows you best. He was just real derogatory in everything he did...when the scouts would come down there, he would lock up the film room and go home! He was just mean to everybody—he's hurt countless players that way."

college *stats*

Season		Rushes	Yards	Catches	Yards	TDs
1991	Long Beach St.	55	262	4	92	3
1992	Georgia	53	388	3	38	4
1993	Georgia	167	824	12	161	8
1994	Georgia	97	445	31	330	6
TOTAL		372	1,919	50	621	21

college *achievements*

Team Rushing Leader 1993
Preseason Second-Team All-SEC 1994
Blue-Gray All-Star Selection 1994

By the time the NFL held its scouting combines the following spring, Terrell was healthy again. He joined hundreds of other hopefuls as they were measured, weighed, timed, and evaluated in every imaginable area. Terrell went in as a long shot and, unfortunately, came out as an even longer shot. His time in the 40-yard dash was 4.7 seconds—a half-second behind many of the runners at the tryouts. "I don't think I had the kind of stats that pro scouts were looking for," Terrell admits. "Scouts looked at me in terms of my tangibles instead of my intangibles."

High on the list of intangibles for Terrell was that he was what football people call a "downhill" runner. In other words, some invisible force always seemed to be pulling him forward. In a sport where an extra few feet on the end of a run can keep a drive alive, this is a very valuable asset. Among Terrell's more *tangible* qualities were his blocking and pass-catching abilities, and his willingness to pound on defenders away from the ball. Luckily, the Denver Broncos noticed these things about Terrell. They decided to take him in the sixth round of the NFL draft and give him a chance.

"When you get drafted this late, all you are is camp meat," says Terrell, referring to the term veterans use for the human tackling dummies taken at the end of the draft. Often they do not survive a team's first cut; if they make it, the odds of these rookies playing more than a minor role on the team once the season starts are slim. But Terrell was determined to show Coach Mike Shanahan that he had gotten the bargain of the draft.

Terrell made sure to hit the right holes on running plays and make good blocks when he had to, and he showed great enthusiasm covering punts and kickoffs. In an exhibition game against the San Francisco 49ers, he hit kickoff returner Tyronne Drakeford while running at full speed. Terrell not only made the tackle, he blasted Drakeford back 15 feet! When he returned to the sideline, a veteran sidled over and told Terrell he would make the opening day roster on that hit alone.

Those words of encouragement were all Terrell needed. He played with the confidence of a first-round pick, and began to get the Denver coaching staff excited. The more they looked at his game, the more they liked him. Terrell was adept at reading blocks, and could squirt through the slimmest of openings without getting knocked off his feet or coughing up the football. He also responded to coaching better than any rookie that had come through Broncos training camp in years. As for Terrell's questionable durability, when he got hit hard, more often than not it was the tacklers who were limping back to the huddle.

Incredibly, by the end of camp, Terrell had not only made the team, he had won the starting job.

"Since he's been here, my job has basically been to pick up third downs, to keep him on the field so I can hand him the ball."
JOHN ELWAY

Busting Loose

chapter 6

"It makes you wonder how many guys have been hidden like that and never got discovered."

— JOHN ELWAY

The first-string halfback for the Denver Broncos in the opening game of the 1995 season was not listed in the *NFL Register*, which has a special section profiling more than 125 of the league's most promising newcomers. That was nothing new. A year earlier, in the University of Georgia media guide, the last paragraph in Terrell's bio began "Soon, Davis will have to move away from football...." By season's end, however, the name Terrell Davis was etched in the NFL record book as the lowest draft choice ever to gain 1,000 yards.

Terrell outgained all but one of the 20 runners drafted ahead of him—including Ki-Jana Carter, Napoleon Kaufman, Rashaan Salaam, James Stewart, and Tyrone Wheatley—and would have beaten them all had he not missed two games to injury. The only rookie to pile up more yards was Curtis Martin of the New England Patriots, one of Terrell's best friends. Martin led the American Football Conference in rushing yards, but Terrell edged him out for the AFC lead in yards per carry, averaging 4.7 every time he touched the ball.

Terrell hits the open field against the Houston Oilers during his rookie year. This 60-yard run was good for one of the eight touchdowns he scored in 1995.

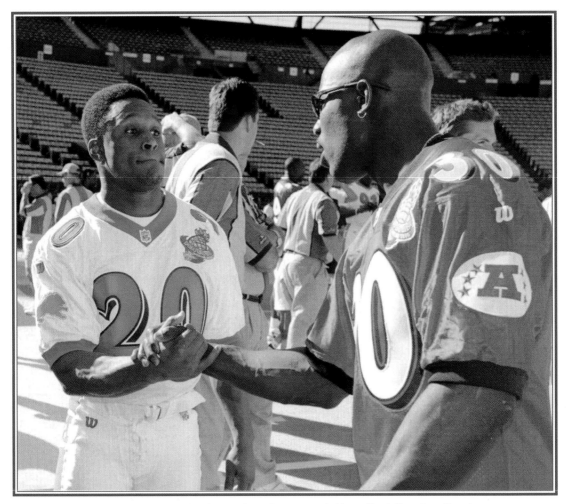

Detroit superstar Barry Sanders greets Terrell at the Pro Bowl.
Sanders edged Terrell for the NFL rushing title in 1996.

Quarterback John Elway was happy to have Terrell in his backfield. Denver's opponents—who used to defend the Broncos by simply unleashing wave upon wave of pass rushers—now had to lay off Elway for fear of what Terrell might do with all that extra running room. With more time to find his receivers (and less time spent in the middle of linebacker sandwiches), the veteran QB picked defenses apart. One of his favorite targets was Terrell, who reeled in 49 passes for 367 yards. The Broncos were so pleased with Terrell that they tore up his three-year, $500,000 contract and handed him a new one worth nearly $7 million.

In the second year of his NFL career, Terrell solidified his status as one of the game's premier running backs. Over the off-season, Coach Shanahan had made two things clear to him. First, he would no longer catch teams by surprise—they would be ready for him in '96. Second, now that he was the team's featured back, he would have to progress quickly in order for the Broncos to make it to the Super Bowl. Elway was in his late 30s and would soon retire. The "window of opportunity" was narrow—if Terrell waited until Elway's successor came on the scene, then *he* would be the aging star desperate to win the big one.

Terrell understood, and he responded with a spectacular year. With defenses now keying on him, he nevertheless continued to produce big games and—more important—big yards when the team desperately needed them. In a high-profile contest against the Patriots, Terrell amassed 154 yards in a 34–8 victory. Against the Baltimore Ravens, he racked up 194 yards to establish a new team record. He finished the year with 1,538 yards, which led the AFC and broke the old team record of 1,407.

After the season's 16th game, Terrell was ahead of Barry Sanders by 160 yards, and thought he had the NFL rushing title wrapped up. But the Lions played their final game the next night, and Detroit coach Wayne Fontes (out of the playoffs and soon to be out of a job) decided to keep handing Sanders the ball until he passed Terrell. "Everyone was congratulating me and telling me that I had won the title, and then Barry put up 175 yards that Monday night and took the crown," smiles Terrell, who joined Sanders as a 1996 NFL All-Pro. "That's all right. Barry Sanders is the best back in the NFL, and I was just happy to have had such a great year."

"We have a high level of respect for him...he's all man."
SHANNON SHARPE

Though spectacular on paper, the 1996 season was not an unqualified success for Terrell. In a September game against the Tampa Bay Buccaneers, he got nailed by linebacker Lonnie Marts and felt one of those headaches coming on. Terrell stayed in the game, but he could barely see, and he was becoming nauseous. After missing a block and dropping a pass, he took himself out. A snort of a medicine called Migrainal enabled Terrell to reenter the game in the second half (and score the winning touchdown), but this was an alarming development. In all the years he had suffered from migraines, not once had one kept him from playing football. Later in the year, against the San Diego Chargers, he experienced identical symptoms after a hit and needed the Migrainal again. He returned to the game, but was sluggish and ineffective.

Terrell was scared. It was different when he was a kid, when he sometimes felt he had nothing to lose. Now the headaches might cost him everything he had worked so hard to achieve.

Terrell went to see a number of specialists, and at their suggestion began to make some changes in his life. He stopped eating chocolate and tried to avoid sodas that contained caffeine. He also began taking vitamin B-6 and magnesium supplements. A chiropractor began working to loosen up the tightness in his neck, and he started wearing braces on his teeth in order to relieve pressure in the back of his mouth. Whenever Terrell felt a migraine coming on, he took his medicine and breathed extra oxygen. The full-fledged attacks stopped, and he finished the year without incident.

Terrell was ready for the postseason, but his teammates were not. Favored by some to reach the Super Bowl, the Broncos took their first-round opponent, the Jacksonville Jaguars, a little too lightly. A second-year expansion team, the Jags had already upset the Buffalo Bills in the Wild Card game, yet were still two-touchdown underdogs against Denver. Things started well enough, with the Broncos scoring twice early. But momentum shifted, the Jacksonville defense shut down Elway, and his counterpart, Mark Brunell, ran the Denver defense ragged. Despite Terrell's 115 yards of offense, the Broncos lost, 30–27.

Terrell and his teammates watched the following week as the Patriots beat Jacksonville by 25 points and advanced to the Super Bowl. Everyone on the team knew that it should have been the Broncos going to the Super Bowl. To a man, they promised themselves they would never waste an opportunity like that again.

Coach's Corner

Here's what Mike Shanahan, head coach of the Denver Broncos, has to say about Terrell:

"Terrell has the soft hands that our offense requires. And when he's not catching the ball, he can be a devastating blocker in passing situations."

"He's absolutely terrific—there's not an ounce of selfishness in him."

"There's not an area in his game that isn't strong."

The Road to San Diego

chapter 7

"He's the best in the NFL."

— **KANSAS CITY CHIEFS COACH, MARTY SCHOTTENHEIMER**

The Denver Broncos were a team on a mission in 1997. They had worked so hard the year before with little to show for their efforts. This year would be different, they vowed, and the experts certainly seemed to agree. The Broncos were a team built to go all the way. The defense, led by safety Steve Atwater and linebacker Bill Romanowski, was experienced and aggressive. On offense, a veteran front line opened up holes for Terrell and pass-blocked for Elway, which meant Denver could strike quickly through the air or grind out tough yards on the ground.

For most of the year, it was a combination of both. Elway threw for a career-best 27 touchdowns and only 11 interceptions. Terrell ran for 1,750 yards and tied for the league lead in touchdowns (15) and points (96). Besides breaking his own franchise record for yards in a season, he also became the first runner in Denver history to reach the 200-yard plateau when he ran for 215 yards against the Cincinnati Bengals.

Marty Schottenheimer

Terrell and his teammates were focused and committed during the 1997 season, winning 9 of their first 10 games.

The only bump in the road for Denver during '97 was a loss to the surprising Pittsburgh Steelers. The defeat prevented the Broncos from winning the Western Division, which meant they would have to go into the playoffs as a Wild Card. The fans were nervous. Although the Broncos had started the year 9–1, they had only managed to split their last six games. The defense was looking old and tired, and the offensive line had not fared well against bigger opponents. The odds were also against them in another respect: Only one Wild Card team in NFL history had ever won the Super Bowl.

The first playoff game, against Jacksonville, was a matter of revenge. Terrell and company buried the Jags, 42–17, with the defense coming through time after time. In the next round, against the Kansas City Chiefs, Denver won a tense battle, 14-10. Again, the defense played tough. Terrell did the bulk of the offensive work in these two games, with a total of 285 rushing yards.

The road to the Super Bowl had just one more obstacle, the Steelers. In their earlier meeting, Coach Shanahan instructed his defense to lay back and wait for young quarterback Kordell Stewart to start making mistakes. Stewart crossed them up by turning in his best game as a pro. This time, the Broncos threw everything but the kitchen sink at Kordell, giving him a different look on every single play. By the second half, he was thoroughly befuddled, and the Broncos managed to gain a three-point edge. Terrell ran out the clock and the Broncos were on their way to San Diego with a hard-earned 24–21 victory.

"You can get a guy in the first round who's one of the biggest busts ever, and you also can end up getting somebody like Terrell."

**BRONCOS GUARD
MARK SCHLERETH**

Simply Super

chapter 8

"The Green Bay defense was not only humiliated, but so exhausted that they literally couldn't play anymore. Terrell Davis did that to them."

— ESPN COMMENTATOR TOM JACKSON

The Broncos and Green Bay Packers squared off in Super Bowl XXXII on January 18, 1998. The last time the two teams had met, a season earlier, Green Bay swamped Denver, 41–6. That, and the fact that the Packers seemed to be head-and-shoulders above any other team in football, made the Broncos a 14-point underdog heading into the game. On paper, the experts trumpeted, the game was "un-winnable" for Denver.

Ironically, it was on *paper* where the Broncos gained an important edge.

Coach Shanahan was schooled in the complexities of NFL offenses while serving as an assistant with the San Francisco 49ers, where he specialized in tailoring game plans to exploit an opponent's weaknesses. Heading into the Super Bowl clash with the Packers, he detected a flaw in Green Bay's defensive alignment—a small glitch that would neutralize cornerback LeRoy Butler and defensive end Reggie White if certain plays were run out of a specific formation. Until the Packers realized what was hap-

Terrell turns the camera on the media prior to Super Bowl XXXII. Reporters asked him all week long how it felt to return to his hometown of San Diego.

pening and could correct this flaw, it would be up to Terrell to pile up as many yards as possible and—more important—wear out the Green Bay defensive line.

Of course, the clever offensive plan would count for nothing if the Broncos' defensive plan failed. And when the game opened it appeared it might. Denver's defense had one goal in this game: Contain quarterback Brett Favre. A three-time MVP, Favre was the kind of player who could make something happen out of nothing. He was a superb dropback passer who became even better when he was forced to run. On the opening drive, Favre engineered a 76-yard touchdown drive to put Green Bay up 7–0.

The Broncos answered, however, with a long drive of their own, with Terrell taking the ball into the end zone from one yard out. The Denver defense then asserted itself, forcing two turnovers, and slowly the momentum began to turn. Then disaster struck. On the final play of the first quarter, with Denver on the verge of a touchdown, Terrell took a knee to the

Did You Know?

In the Broncos' previous three Super Bowls, their runners gained a total of just 213 yards. Terrell got 259 in Super Bowls XXXII and XXXIII.

head from Butler. The gun sounded, signaling the players to switch ends of the field. When Terrell turned to start walking, his vision started to go. He had made it through the entire season without an episode, but he could tell that this was going to be a bad one. "I was like, *Not today man!*" he says.

Brian Williams comes up with an armful of air as Terrell dodges another Packer.
By game's end, the Green Bay defense was exhausted.

He staggered to the bench for some oxygen and some Migrainal when he heard Coach Shanahan calling him. The ball was on the one-yard line, and he needed Terrell in the game. He informed Shanahan he could not see, but the coach asked him if he

Terrell celebrates one of his record three Super Bowl touchdowns.

could go in and pretend to take a handoff. The idea was for Terrell to draw Green Bay's attention by jumping up and over the pile while Elway hid the ball on his hip and pranced untouched into the end zone. "I wasn't going to argue," Terrell recalls, "but I told him, As long as you know I can't *see*."

As Terrell said later, he had run that play so many times that he could do it with his eyes shut. In this case, he *did*. Elway took the snap, faked the hand-off, and the entire Packer defense went after Terrell. Elway scored untouched. The invincible Green Bay defense looked pretty stupid going after a blind man who did not even have the football!

Terrell's sacrifice gave his teammates a huge boost. And they would need it, for he was unable to play for the rest of the first half. He gulped down oxygen and prayed for the medication to kick in. The Broncos went into the locker room leading 17–14 and feeling good. They came out feeling unbeatable: Terrell announced he was well enough to play.

On Denver's first possession, Shanahan was surprised to see that the Packers had not figured out his offensive plan, and thus had not made any adjustments for the second half. Perhaps because Terrell sat out the second quarter and Denver had trouble moving the ball, Green Bay defensive coordinator Fritz Shurmur did not feel there was a weakness *being* exploited. In the battle of the Xs and Os, this proved to be the decisive error. With the Broncos running game back at full strength and the Packer defense starting to gasp for breath, the game was about to turn.

After Green Bay booted a field goal to tie the game at 17–17, the second half was all Terrell. Running out of Shanahan's special set, he flashed through the line, cut back against the grain, and turned the corner play after play after play. He chewed up the clock and kept his defensive teammates off the field, while the Green Bay defense became more and more exhausted. White, perhaps the greatest defensive end ever to play, was barely a factor. Gilbert Brown, the Packers' monster in the middle, was so tired that he could do little more than wave at Terrell as he barreled past him. And every time Green Bay tried to clamp down on the run, Elway fired a ball downfield to stretch the defense out. It was a magnificent plan, executed perfectly. Terrell pounded the ball into the end zone again, giving the Broncos a 24–17 lead.

The Packers, however, were not about to roll over—a great team finds ways to stay alive. At the end of the third quarter, for instance, the Broncos had an excellent chance to put the game away. But Green Bay's Eugene Robinson picked off an Elway pass in the end zone to keep his team within a touchdown. Then Favre went to work. He took his team down the field and hit Antonio Freeman with a 13-yard pass to knot the game at 24–24.

The Davis File

TERRELL'S FAVORITE...

Video Game . . . Madden Football '99
Music . . . . R&B and Rap
Ice Cream . . . . Vanilla
Soda . . . . Decaffeinated cola
Commercial . . . . Campbell's Chunky Soup (starring Terrell)
Number . . . . 7 (his number at Lincoln Prep)
Book . . . Dreams in Motion (by Terrell)
Sport . . . . Bowling
Actors . . . . Martin Lawrence and Stacey Dash
Dessert . . . . Cheesecake
Animal . . . . Alligator

Terrell and Novartis Pharmaceuticals teamed up in 1998 to create *The Terrell Davis Foundation for Migraine Education and Treatment.* Terrell wants migraine sufferers to know they are not alone, and that they can reach their goals with the right treatment and support.

Terrell gives a teammate his trademark salute during Super Bowl XXXII.

The Broncos started their final drive from midfield, with three-and-a-half minutes left. This was the knockout blow Shanahan and his coaching staff had planned. Denver got to the 32-yard line when Darius Holland was whistled for tackling Terrell by his facemask. Then Elway hit Howard Griffith with a short swing pass. The fullback had been throwing great blocks for Terrell all game long, and now it was his chance to shine. He wriggled his way downfield for a 23-yard gain. The Packers stood tough on the next two plays, setting up third down with six yards to go. Elway faded back to pass but could not find an open receiver. An interception would have been disastrous at this stage, so he tucked the ball under his arm and ran right into the teeth of the Green Bay defense. As Elway approached the first-down marker, Butler came barreling toward him. The Packers safety went low, and Elway went high. Butler clipped his legs and spun him around like a helicopter, then Mike Prior nailed Elway while he was spinning in the air. Somehow, the quarterback held on to the ball after his suicidal run. A holding penalty on Shannon Sharpe pushed Denver back 10 yards, but Terrell scissored through the defense for 17 yards. He then burst into the end zone for his third one-yard touchdown run of the day. The score was 31–24. A minute and 15 seconds later, the Broncos were NFL champions.

After the game, Terrell was named Super Bowl MVP. He had gained 157 yards and scored three touchdowns despite missing all but one play of the second quarter. John Elway, who finally had the one thing missing from his outstanding career, wanted everyone to know how the Broncos did it. Terrell was the man. "We got here on his back," Elway announced in the locker room.

pro stats

Season	Rushes	Yards	Catches	Yards	TDs
1995	237	1,117	49	367	8
1996	345*	1,538*	36	310	15
1997	369	1,750*	42	287	15**
1998	392	2,008***	25	217	23

*LED AFC   **TIED FOR NFL LEAD   ***LED NFL

pro achievements

Runner-Up NFL Rookie of the Year	1995
AFC Yards–Per–Carry Leader	1995, 1998
Pro Bowl Selection	1996, 1997, 1998
NFL All-Pro	1996, 1997, 1998
AFC Rushing Leader	1996, 1997, 1998
NFL Touchdown Leader	1998
NFL Rushing Leader	1998
Most Consecutive 100-yard Postseason Games	1999
Most Rushing TDs in a Super Bowl	1998
Super Bowl XXXII MVP	1998
NFL MVP	1998

Terrell holds the Lombardi Trophy aloft after beating the Packers.
Two weeks later he hit the training room to prepare for the 1998 season.

chapter 9

Staying on Top

*"I'm not quick.
I have subtle moves.
But I think I get
the job done."*
— TERRELL DAVIS

One of the most difficult challenges in any sport is defending a championship. Every team you play the following season tries extra hard to beat you, and sometimes you "beat yourself" by forgetting to do the little things that made you champion in the first place. The Broncos entered the 1998 season favored to return to the Super Bowl. After contemplating retirement, John Elway decided to come back for another year. The rest of the Denver players were healthy and focused. As for Terrell, he was being hailed by some as the best player in football.

Coach Shanahan was hoping for another strong year from his star running back. Terrell had bigger plans. He had learned a lot about the game and about himself, and now he wanted to put that knowledge to use and become a "complete" player. He believed he could dominate football games by probing the defense in the first half, then battering their weak points in the second half—the perfect combination of brains and

No one was happier than Terrell when John Elway decided to return for the 1998 campaign. Rarely have a quarterback and running back worked so well together.

brute strength. The key was to boost his intensity at the same time that opponents were beginning to wear out. This meant Terrell had to strengthen his legs and increase his stamina with regular workouts. The problem was that, in the months following the Super Bowl, Terrell was very busy with interviews, commercials, and public appearances. "One thing I always did was make time to work out, even if it was in a hotel gym someplace," he says. "I started preparing a couple of weeks after the Super Bowl and didn't miss a workout. That was important to me."

When the 1998 season finally opened, no one had any idea how much better Terrell had become—or how much better he would make the Broncos. Over the first 13 games, the team was unbeatable, going 13–0.

Everyone knew Terrell was going to get the ball, yet no one seemed able to stop him. He would take the handoff from Elway, pick a hole, and then explode through it—often dragging a couple of tacklers with him. And, just as Terrell had planned, he was actually running stronger in the fourth quarter, when it counted most. With three games to go, he was closing in on 2,000 rushing yards, a total reached by just three other players in NFL history.

In the next two games, Denver's opponents—the Giants and Dolphins—tried a new strategy. They sent everyone after Terrell and dared Elway to beat them with his passing. The ploy caught the Broncos off guard and both games ended in defeat.

Did You Know?

Terrell bought his mother a house down the street in suburban Denver. His brothers still live in San Diego, but visit him during the off-season.

In the final week of the season, Denver played the Seattle Seahawks. Terrell now needed a tremendous game in order to top 2,000 yards. The team pulled together and played like a champion. And Terrell chewed up the Seahawks for 178 yards to finish with a league-best 2,008. It was a monumental achievement—to everyone except Terrell. "With John back there throwing the ball," he says modestly, "anybody could run for 2,000 yards."

In the divisional playoff, the Broncos avenged their loss to the Miami Dolphins, trouncing them 38–3. Terrell let the Dolphins pursue him as they had in the previous game, but employed his great cutback move, with deadly effectiveness. Just when Miami thought they had cornered Terrell, he would slice sideways "against the grain" and romp into the defensive secondary. He finished with 199 yards. Against the Jets in the AFC Championship, the Broncos played a sloppy first half , but recovered to score three second-half touchdowns when the game hung in the balance. After that, it was T.D. Time, as Terrell barreled for first down after first down against the overmatched Jets. He finished with 167 yards in Denver's 23–10 victory. Terrell had equaled an NFL mark with his sixth consecutive 100-yard postseason game. Records mattered little, however—he was thrilled about going back to the Super Bowl!

Terrell cuts back against the Jets in the AFC Championship. His solid performance proved the difference in a mistake-filled game.

Atlanta coach Dan Reeves instructed his players to swarm around Terrell during Super Bowl XXXIII, yet he still managed to gain more than 100 yards.

Denver's Super Bowl XXXIII opponent, the Atlanta Falcons, presented an interesting challenge. They were a mirror image of the Broncos. The Falcons had a superb running game, a veteran quarterback, talented receivers, a fast, aggressive defense, and terrific special teams. The main difference between the two teams was experience; the Broncos had been in this position before, while the Falcons had never come close.

Coach Shanahan decided to capitalize on Atlanta's inexperience and sent waves of blitzing defenders at quarterback Chris Chandler whenever the Falcons got close to the end zone. The Falcons, who were piloted by ex-Bronco head coach Dan Reeves, decided to try the only strategy that had beaten Denver in 1998. The defense keyed on Terrell and dared Elway to beat them.

When All-Pro tight end Shannon Sharpe had to leave the game in the first quarter with a knee injury, it looked as if Reeves's plan might work. But on this day, Elway was up to the challenge. He went right at the Falcons and picked their secondary apart, amassing 336 passing yards. Atlanta never wavered, however, stubbornly focusing their attention on Terrell. Three times in the second half, they went after him in goal-line situations only to find that he was merely a decoy. Blocking fullback Howard Griffith scored two touchdowns on these plays, and Elway kept the ball himself on a third. The final score was 34–19. Terrell took control at the end, running out the clock and gaining enough ground to break the 100-yard mark for a record seventh straight game. For only the fifth time in history, a team had won back-to-back Super Bowls.

Terrell stretches prior to the big game against the Falcons.

Terrell "runs downhill" against Atlanta, barreling through a tackle attempt by Chuck Smith.

"I just hope that when I'm finished playing I will have meant as much to this team as John has."

— TERRELL DAVIS

A day after their Super Bowl XXXIII victory, Terrell and John Elway still can't wipe the smiles off their faces.

Terrell's Team

"He's always seemed to be the player who was overlooked. All this has taken him by surprise."
— **KATEREE DAVIS**

lthough Denver's Super Bowl wins have been the crowning achievement in John Elway's fabulous career, the Broncos were Terrell's team in 1997 and 1998. Although he would never admit it, deep down he knows it is true. Certainly, where they go from here will depend on him.

Many players would shrink from this responsibility. But Terrell welcomes it. For the guy whom no one ever paid attention to, it is a welcome change of pace. "I've never been the go-to guy, I've never been on a team where everybody looked at me as one of their weapons," he explains. "This is the first time ever that I have felt wanted, where I have been an integral part of an offense, a team...I welcome that type of pressure."

Actually, Terrell claims all those years he was ignored have turned out to be a blessing in disguise. Unlike his NFL peers, he has not carried the ball 300 times a season since he was 15 years old. Until he reached the pros, the only time he was a "workhorse" was way back in Pop Warner. Getting buried in high school and college may have made it tougher to get noticed, but now he is reaping the benefits. "For a while I thought that it hurt my chances of making it in the pros," Terrell explains. "But now I see that it didn't. Maybe it even saved my legs."

Another advantage of being a "nobody" for so long is that, until recently, Terrell was able to walk the streets unnoticed. Not anymore. He has become one of Denver's most recognizable celebrities, and is mobbed whenever he shows his face. "I'm not used to having to walk around and hide!" he laughs. Luckily, Terrell is strictly a "stay-at-home" guy. An evening of video games, music, good food, friends, and family is all the excitement he can stand these days.

> ## Did You Know?
>
> In the off-season, Terrell concentrates on workouts that will help his durability, not his size. Unlike most NFL players, he lifts weights just to stay in shape—his real training is running, taking care of his body, and watching what he eats.

When Terrell does brave the crowds, it's usually for a good cause. After Super Bowl XXXII, he formed the Terrell Davis Foundation for Migraine Education and Treatment. Between games and during the off-season, he meets with migraine sufferers of all ages to let them know they're not alone, and that a cure could soon be on the way.

In the eyes of many, Terrell has become the perfect NFL runner. He jackhammers defenses all game long, doling out as much punishment as he absorbs. And when an opponent is properly softened up, he is primed to deliver the knockout blow. Terrell, however, will be the first to tell you that he has started his career in the perfect situation. The Broncos offense has featured excellent receivers, smart and agile blockers, an offensive genius for a coach, and one of the greatest quarterbacks ever. In Terrell's mind, he is simply doing his job.

What is important to Terrell? He has given this matter a great deal of thought. When the day comes that he must take off his pads and hang up his cleats, he wants to walk away from football knowing he has left a little bit of himself behind. "I want to leave my signature on the game," says Terrell, who adds that this has little to do with personal records and achievements. "The way you do that is by winning championships. Because ultimately this is a team game."

> "Don't give up. I say that with conviction. It happened to me. When people told me I couldn't do it, I didn't listen. Don't give up!"
> TERRELL DAVIS (WITH JAY LENO ON "THE TONIGHT SHOW WITH JAY LENO")

Index

PAGE NUMBERS IN ITALICS REFER TO ILLUSTRATIONS.